ALL THE BEST CHICKEN DINNERS

ALL THE BEST

CHICKEN DINNERS

BY

JOIE WARNER

HEARST BOOKS • New York

A FLAVOR BOOK

LIBRARY OF CONGRESS CATALOGING-IN-PUBLICATION DATA
Warner, Joie.
    All the best chicken dinners/by Joie Warner.
        p.   cm.
Includes index.
ISBN 0-688-11657-4
1. Cookery (Chicken).   I. Title.   II. Title: Chicken
Dinners.
TX750.5.C45W37   1992
641.6′65-dc20   92-14208
                                                              CIP

Printed in the United States of America
First Edition
1 2 3 4 5 6 7 8 9 10

This book was created and produced by

Flavor Publications, Inc.
208 East 51st Street, Suite 240
New York, New York 10022

CONTENTS

INTRODUCTION

THERE'S NO DOUBT about it, great-tasting, good-for-you chicken is America's favorite entrée. And it's no wonder. Whether chile-rubbed or simply stewed, chicken is the most versatile meat with its affinity for so many flavor combinations and seasonings. Chicken is universally enjoyed around the world, served either deluxe or down-home; hot or cold; simply grilled or swiftly sautéed, with or without a sauce; skinned, boned, or stuffed, whole or in parts – even leftovers are easily transformed into wonderful dishes. Yes, it is true, you can eat chicken every day and never, ever tire of it.

Chicken is the most economical meat you can purchase. But, best of all, it's low-fat and low-calorie – as long as you prepare chicken in ways that don't add fat or calories and you discard the skin which contains almost half of chicken's saturated fat. The good news is that it is perfectly fine to keep the skin on when broiling or roasting rather than removing it before cooking as so many dietitians and nutritionists have been advocating in recent years. Keeping the skin intact during cooking, then removing it before eating, helps to keep the meat wonderfully moist and flavorful. (Now, that doesn't mean that some of us nondieters cannot indulge occasionally in crispy-skinned fried chicken and the like – at least that is my philosophy!) Also, to further reduce calories from soups and stews, remove the fat at the opening of the chicken's cavity and skim off most of the surface fat (keeping a little fat for flavor). This is most easily done by first chilling the finished stew, soup, or stock so that the fat rises to the top for easy removal.

Chicken is nutritious – an excellent source of protein, vitamins A, thiamine, niacin, riboflavin and the minerals iron, zinc, phosphorous, and calcium.

Chicken is easy to cook. As every accomplished cook knows, simply baking or grilling chicken, with only a modest adornment of a few herbs or spices is, without a doubt, the tastiest, healthiest and, happily, the most uncomplicated way to prepare chicken. It is good to know that fancy techniques and complex sauces do nothing to enhance chicken's flavor. Unpretentious, straightforward preparations are almost always best. And, though fresh chicken is readily available in supermarkets and butcher shops everywhere, if your freezer is well stocked with boneless and bone-in chicken breasts, as well as thighs or a cut-up fryer, you will always be prepared for spur-of-the-moment cooking.

But what I really love most about chicken is its marvelous affinity for teaming with nutritious grains, pastas, and beans, such as couscous or rice. As well, chicken combines with an endless variety of fresh vegetables, and with fruit.

The recipes that follow are mostly quick and simple – many taking only ten minutes to prepare – and many can be prepared ahead and reheated. Some recipes are low-calorie and some use cream and butter because I like their flavor. You, on the other hand, should feel free to reduce calories at will by substituting olive oil for butter or low-fat versions of sour cream or half-and-half for heavy cream. The same goes for salt. In many recipes I specify the amount of salt necessary to bring out the flavor, but if you are on a salt-reduced diet, then omit it altogether or add to taste. I also adore the taste of garlic, black pepper, herbs, and spices and use them generously.

I hope you will find many delicious ideas for everyday suppers and special occasions in this book. I've included my rendition of American classics as well as treasured recipes from around the world. I've arranged the chapters into sections – Chicken Breasts; Chicken Thighs, Legs, and Wings; Ground Chicken; Whole and

Cut-Up Chicken; and Accompaniments because I usually plan my menu around what looks fresh at the market that day or what I have in my larder rather than by cooking method. I have suggested what to serve with what, but for goodness' sake, use your own imagination and combine some of my ideas with your own. You'll notice that I suggest rice or grains with many dishes. It's not that I'm stuck in a rut, it's just that I simply adore rice and grains.

You will also notice that I haven't included any dessert recipes in this book. If, and when, I serve dessert, it is usually something very simple such as fresh fruit.

Above all, I hope this book will give as much pleasure to you in using these recipes as I have enjoyed in creating them.

JOIE WARNER

◆ ◆ ◆

BASICS

BUYING CHICKEN

So what's better – supermarket or free-range chicken? Range-fed or free-range chickens have been allowed to roam – usually around a small barnyard – and eat freely. These chickens are fed a more varied diet with less drugs than regular chicken, giving their meat more texture and flavor. While not quite as tender as supermarket chicken, they are far superior. Most – but not all – supermarket chicken is mass produced, bland tasting, and has a mushy texture. Some savvy supermarkets do offer premium-quality chicken – you'll notice brand names on the wrapping. Since locally produced premium brands aren't available nationwide, it is impossible to give recommendations. Just remember that not all brands are of superior quality. It is up to you to ignore advertising claims and to try different brands until you find one that consistently pleases you.

Always purchase fresh, never frozen chicken with a fresh, clean aroma. Fresh chicken has moist, unbroken skin, with no bruising, red splotches, or odor. Check the expiration date, and give it good sniff through the plastic wrap before bringing it home. Avoid chicken with too much liquid in the package or torn packaging.

STORING CHICKEN

Once home, remove the chicken from the packaging, rinse, and pat dry with paper towels. Rewrap in plastic wrap (I always double wrap), foil, or freezer bags and store in the coldest part of the refrigerator for no more than two days or in the freezer for longer storage. Never refreeze chicken if previously frozen and thawed. Whole chicken will last up to two to three months in the freezer; chicken parts and ground chicken up to one month. Most charts for freezer storage allow for up to one year for a whole chicken and six months for chicken parts, but I'm very finicky and find that any food frozen for any length of time gets "freezer flavor." I personally prefer to purchase chicken and cook it the same day, though I usually purchase extra to freeze for inevitable emergencies.

THAWING AND HANDLING CHICKEN

Do not unwrap the chicken from its freezer package. Once thawed, it should be cooked as soon as possible. The refrigerator is the safest place to thaw, allowing about five hours per pound. For quicker thawing, place chicken in a plastic bag and immerse in cold water, allowing about one hour per pound for thawing, changing the water occasionally.

Recently, we have been warned about the potential health risks of eating chicken that might harbor salmonella. If care is taken when handling and cooking chicken, then we can be assured that the bacteria have been completely destroyed.

Always cook chicken to the well-done stage – never rare or medium. Salmonella is killed at a temperature of 140°F but it is recommended that poultry be cooked to 160°F on boneless parts and 180°F at the thigh. Properly cooked chicken shows no pink and juices run clear. Thoroughly wash hands, utensils, and surfaces that have come into contact with raw chicken with hot, soapy water. It is more frequently raw chicken juices that are the culprit in contaminating other uncooked foods, not undercooked chicken.

TYPES OF CHICKEN

The taste and texture of poultry is affected by its size. Younger chickens weighing from 2 to 4 pounds are the most tender and versatile. Marketed as broiler/fryers (also called simply broiler or fryer), they are best for broiling, roasting, barbecuing, poaching, and sautéing.

Roasters usually weigh between 4 and 7 pounds and are best for baking. Older birds, called stewing chickens or hens, are best for stewing, braising, and poaching because they are tougher, but they have plenty of flavor. Rock Cornish Game Hens are about 1 to 1½ pounds and are best baked and split-roasted, grilled, or broiled. Unfortunately, because they are usually only available frozen, I rarely serve them. Capons are castrated roosters weighing 4 to 8 pounds that have an abundance of tender, juicy white meat. They are perfect for stuffing and roasting.

White meat versus dark meat: white is leaner, but dark meat is much more flavorful and more moist – definitely my preference.

White meat is perfect for in-a-hurry and last-minute cooking, which is probably why it's the choice of today's busy cooks. Dark meat is the most versatile, remaining moist and juicy when braised, stewed, stir-fried, grilled, broiled, or roasted. Ground chicken is now readily available in supermarkets and butcher shops which is a terrific low-fat, low-cholesterol alternative to beef burgers and meatloaf – or any dish where you would usually use ground beef.

INGREDIENTS

BASIL: Thai basil is a variety used in Southeast Asian cooking. It's available in Asian grocery stores. If unavailable, substitute any fresh basil. In any recipe calling for fresh basil, do not substitute dried.

BLACK OLIVES: I use Kalamata olives from Greece in my recipes. You may also use Niçoise olives from France. They are available in specialty food shops and many supermarkets. Canned American olives do not have the flavor or pungency needed for the recipes in this book.

BLACK PEPPER: I always use freshly ground black peppercorns.

CAPERS: These are the unopened flower buds of a Mediterranean shrub. Many cooks recommend the tiny French capers which are wonderful for uncooked dishes. But for cooking, I prefer the large assertively-flavored variety. They are packed in vinegar (not salt), and I never rinse them.

CARIBBEAN HOT SAUCE: An extraordinarily hot, distinctively flavored chile sauce made from the hottest pepper in the world – the habanero – also known as Scotch bonnet peppers. Use the red-colored sauce – not the yellow – in these recipes. There is no substitute for Caribbean hot sauce. It's available in Caribbean food shops.

CELLOPHANE NOODLES: Also called bean thread noodles, these dry white noodles are made from mung bean starch. They become soft and gelatinous when soaked. The brand I purchase (Lungkow Vermicelli (Bean Thread)) consists of several small cellophane packages that are encased in pink plastic webbing. It's available in Asian food stores.

CHINESE BLACK MUSHROOMS: These are dried shiitake mushrooms which are available in Asian food shops. They must be reconstituted in hot water before use.

CHICKEN STOCK: Homemade is best, but canned (diluted) is perfectly acceptable. Do not use chicken bouillon cubes.

COCONUT MILK: This is the liquid obtained from pressing the coconut flesh, not the liquid found inside the coconut. I use the unsweetened canned coconut milk (not the sweetened coconut cream for drinks). The best coconut milk comes from Thailand. The brand I use has a picture of a measuring cup and a coconut on the label. It's available in Asian food stores.

CORIANDER: A pungently aromatic herb also known as cilantro or Chinese parsley. It's available in Asian and Latin American food shops, some supermarkets, and produce stores.

DRIED HERBS: The fresher the dried herbs, the more flavorful your food. Bottled herbs that have lost their color and aroma should be replaced.

FISH SAUCE: The Thai name for this fermented fish sauce is nam pla. It's used as a condiment and ingredient in Southeast Asian cooking. A good quality sauce is "Squid" brand. It's available in Asian food shops.

FLOUR TORTILLAS: Available at most supermarkets.

GARLIC: It is hard to imagine anyone not cooking with garlic (lots of it!), for it is a seasoning that goes with almost every savory dish. Choose large bulbs that are tightly closed and not sprouting. Squeeze the bulb to make sure it is firm and fresh. Powdered garlic should be avoided in any recipe calling for fresh garlic though it is perfectly acceptable when used with other dried herbs in seasoning mixes for "dry" marinades.

GINGER: Always use fresh ginger unless otherwise specified. Powdered ginger and fresh ginger aren't interchangeable. Select young ginger with smooth, shiny skin. Ginger lasts for months in the refrigerator if first wrapped in a paper towel, then placed in a plastic bag. The paper towel must be replaced often: the ginger will become moldy otherwise.

GOAT CHEESE: For the recipes in this book, I use the fresh, soft, mild-tasting variety. Goat cheese is available at most supermarkets and cheese shops.

JALAPEÑOS: I use the canned pickled or brine-packed variety for the recipes in this book. They are available at most supermarkets in the Mexican food section.

MONTEREY JACK CHEESE: Sort of a cross between Cheddar and mozzarella cheese with excellent melting qualities. It is available in most supermarkets and specialty cheese shops.

PARMESAN: Be sure to purchase Parmesan that has the words "Parmigiano Reggiano" or second best, "Grana Padano" stamped on the rind. Always grate it fresh just before using: it begins to lose flavor after grating. It is available in Italian food shops or well-stocked cheese stores.

PLANTAIN: A cousin to the banana, it must be cooked before eating. Plantains are found in Caribbean and Latin American food shops and some supermarkets.

SAMBAL OELEK: This bottled preparation of crushed red peppers is deliciously hot. Though an Indonesian condiment, I freely use it as a flavoring in other cuisines, too. There really isn't an equal substitute except, maybe, hot red pepper flakes – though red pepper flakes merely add heat whereas sambal oelek imparts delicious flavor as well. It's available in Asian food shops and lasts for quite a long time in the refrigerator.

SOY SAUCE: I use Pearl River Superior brand Chinese soy sauce for the Chinese recipes in this book and Kikkoman brand for Japanese recipes. Both are available in Asian food stores. Please don't use domestic brands that are chemically, not naturally, fermented.

SUN-DRIED TOMATOES: Salty, with an intense flavor of tomatoes, the best ones are imported from Italy – though there are some quality domestic varieties. Sun-dried tomatoes are available in most specialty and Italian food stores. They are available dry-packed or in oil, in jars. Dry-packed should be aromatic and somewhat pliable – not hard and brown – and reddish colored. Before use, place dry-packed tomatoes in a footed strainer and pour boiling water over to soften them. Pack in sterilized jars and cover with olive oil. You may also add a garlic clove, some oregano, and black peppercorns for added flavor. Store in the refrigerator, but bring back to room temperature before using.

THAI RICE: A white, long-grain rice with a delicate jasmine aroma. It's available in some Asian food stores. If unavailable, substitute Basmati or white, long-grain rice.

TOMATOES, FRESH: In the summer I cook with fresh, ripe, unwaxed, regular tomatoes. At other times of the year, I purchase cherry or plum tomatoes which, if left at room temperature to ripen, have more flavor than out-of-season tomatoes. Always leave them at room temperature for best flavor; don't refrigerate unless they begin to overripen.

VERMOUTH: I use dry white French vermouth in my recipes instead of dry white wine. You may substitute dry white wine, of course.

ZEST: The colored outer layer of skin on a citrus fruit.

◆ ◆ ◆

CHICKEN BREASTS

◆ ◆ ◆

Tender chicken replaces the traditional veal in this lemony-tart Italian dish. ◆ A word of warning: this is very lemony – just the way I love it! Reduce the amount of lemon juice if you wish. ◆ Serve with Green Beans with Coarse-Grained Mustard (page 77), and/or Wild Rice (page 89), or Orzo with Parmesan Cheese (page 86).

CHICKEN PICCATA

4 skinless, boneless
  chicken breast halves
¼ cup all-purpose flour
Salt
Freshly ground black
  pepper
2 tablespoons butter
1 tablespoon vegetable oil
1 large garlic clove, finely
  chopped

¼ cup fresh lemon juice
¼ cup dry white vermouth
Thin lemon slices (garnish)
Capers (garnish)
Several very thin slivers
  sweet red pepper
  (optional garnish)

BETWEEN TWO PIECES of plastic wrap, pound chicken breasts with smooth mallet or rolling pin to flatten to ¼-inch thickness.

Combine flour, salt, and pepper on piece of wax paper. Coat chicken with seasoned flour, shaking off excess.

Melt butter with oil in large nonstick skillet over medium-high heat. Add garlic and cook for 1 minute or until tender. Add chicken and cook for 4 minutes each side or until golden brown and just cooked through. Pour lemon juice over chicken, then remove chicken to warmed plates; keep warm.

Pour vermouth into skillet, turn heat to high and cook until slightly thickened, about 2 minutes. Pour over chicken, garnish with lemons, capers, and red pepper slivers. Serves 4.

CHICKEN CURRY WITH FRESH BASIL

4 skinless, boneless
  chicken breast halves
¼ cup all-purpose flour
Salt
Freshly ground black
  pepper
4 tablespoons butter
2 large garlic cloves,
  chopped
6 tablespoons best-quality
  curry powder, or to taste
2 large ripe tomatoes (about
  1 pound), peeled and
  finely chopped
Grated zest of 1 small
  lemon
1 cup heavy cream
½ cup shredded fresh basil
  leaves
Desiccated coconut
  (garnish)
Raisins (garnish)
Granny Smith apple,
  unpeeled, chopped, and
  tossed with a little lemon
  juice (garnish)

BETWEEN TWO PIECES of plastic wrap, pound chicken breasts with smooth mallet or rolling pin to ¼-inch thickness.

Combine flour, salt, and pepper on piece of wax paper. Coat chicken with seasoned flour, shaking off excess.

Melt 2 tablespoons butter in large nonstick skillet over medium-high heat. Add chicken and cook for 4 minutes each side or until golden brown and just cooked through; do not overcook. Remove to a plate.

In same skillet, melt remaining butter over medium heat. Add garlic and cook for 1 minute. Stir in curry powder, tomatoes, lemon zest, salt, and pepper and cook for 3 minutes or until tomato is soft. Stir in cream and cook for 4 minutes or until slightly thickened. Return chicken to sauce, sprinkle in basil, and reheat. Transfer to warm dinner plates and sprinkle with a little coconut, raisins, and apples; serve additional garnishes in separate small bowls. Serves 4.

T*his exquisitely simple chicken dish, beautifully accented with curry and fresh basil, is a dish I like* very much! ◆ *The perfect accompaniment: White Rice (page 88); and perhaps a salad of delicate greens.* ◆ *Need I tell you to use nothing but best-quality curry powder, ripe and flavorful tomatoes, and fresh, fragrant basil?*

Hot red pepper jelly – a South-western condiment – is now available in many super-markets and most gourmet shops. Here it glazes and spikes chicken breasts stuffed with rich-tasting goat cheese. ◆ Serve with a steamed green vegetable – such as asparagus – and crusty French bread.

CHICKEN BREASTS WITH GOAT CHEESE AND RED PEPPER GLAZE

4 boneless chicken breast halves, with skin on
4 ounces soft mild goat cheese, at room temperature
Salt
Freshly ground black pepper
⅓ cup hot red pepper jelly

PREHEAT OVEN to 400°F.

Loosen skin from one side of each chicken breast; stuff equal amounts of goat cheese under skin of each, pressing edges down to keep filling in while baking.

Place chicken skin side up in small baking dish and form them into mound shapes. Sprinkle with salt and pepper. Spread red pepper jelly over chicken – if jelly needs to soften to spreading consistency, warm for a few minutes in small saucepan over medium heat or in the microwave for a few seconds. Bake for 20 to 30 minutes, basting frequently with pan juices, or until chicken is golden brown and cooked through. Serves 4.

CHICKEN BREASTS STUFFED WITH GARLIC, PARSLEY, AND LEEKS

4 large garlic cloves, finely
  chopped
¾ cup finely chopped
  parsley
¾ cup finely chopped
  white part of leeks;
  previously well rinsed

1 teaspoon very coarsely
  ground (cracked) black
  pepper
Salt
4 tablespoons butter, at
  room temperature
4 chicken breast halves

PREHEAT OVEN to 400°F.

Combine garlic, parsley, leeks, pepper, salt, and butter in bowl. Loosen skin from one side of each chicken breast; stuff equal amounts of butter mixture under skin of each, pressing edges down to keep filling in while baking. Sprinkle with a little salt and pepper and place skin side up in small baking dish. Bake for 30 minutes or until golden brown and cooked through. Serves 2 to 4.

Since I usually have all the ingredients in my pantry, this has become one of my spur-of-the-moment dinners. ♦ Take care to finely chop the vegetables — especially the leeks — or they will be undercooked when the chicken is ready. ♦ Serve with Oven-Fried Potatoes (page 78), and steamed broccoli or green beans.

Chicken breasts coated with a spicy bread-crumb-herb mixture are simply superb. Chicken thighs, legs, drumsticks, and wings are just as delicious and can be substituted for chicken breasts, if desired, or use a combination. ◆ The skin is removed (except chicken wings) before coating with the crumb mixture. ◆ Serve with a salad (see Index) or Corn, Tomato, and Chile Salsa (page 87) and/or a baked potato with sour cream.

HERB BAKED CHICKEN

4 chicken breast halves
½ cup fine dry bread
　crumbs
2 teaspoons dried thyme
1 teaspoon dried tarragon
1 teaspoon salt
½ teaspoon cayenne

½ teaspoon freshly ground
　black pepper
1 large egg
¼ cup milk
¼ cup (2 ounces/½ stick)
　butter, melted

PREHEAT OVEN to 425°F.

　Remove skin from chicken. Combine bread crumbs, thyme, tarragon, salt, cayenne, and pepper on large piece of wax paper. Whisk egg and milk in wide bowl. Dip chicken into egg mixture, then coat in seasoned bread crumbs. Place chicken on rack in baking dish and drizzle with melted butter. Bake for 30 minutes or until cooked through. Serves 2 to 4.

CHICKEN BREASTS WITH GREEN CHILE BUTTER

1 garlic clove
2 green onions (green part only), coarsely chopped
2 tablespoons pickled sliced jalapeños
¼ cup (2 ounces/½ stick) butter, at room temperature

¼ cup (2 ounces) cream cheese, at room temperature
½ teaspoon dried oregano
¼ teaspoon salt
4 boneless chicken breast halves, with skin on

PREHEAT OVEN to 400°F.

Chop garlic and green onions in food processor. Add chiles, butter, cream cheese, oregano, and salt and process until smooth.

Loosen skin from one side of each breast and stuff about a heaping tablespoon butter mixture under skin of each, tucking skin over filling and forming chicken into mound shapes. Place in small baking dish and spread a little of remaining butter over chicken (there will be leftover butter). Bake for 20 minutes or just until cooked through. Serves 4.

Zippy green chile butter stuffed under the skin gives chicken heat and wonderful flavor pizazz. ◆ You can prepare the butter and stuff the chicken several hours in advance, and chill. Besides being very convenient, it adds even more chile flavor. ◆ A spicy meal can be made even more spicy if accompanied by Baked Rice with Cheese and Chiles (page 90). Or serve with Corn, Tomato, and Chile Salsa (page 87). ◆ Any leftover chile butter is delicious spread on boiled corn, with green beans, grilled fish, or new potatoes or you can stuff more chicken breasts if you wish.

C

hicken cooked in a rich
tomato- and tarragon-
flavored sauce is a special
yet undemanding dish. ◆
Buttered egg noodles or plain white rice
and tiny green peas are the perfect
accompaniments.

CHICKEN BREASTS IN
TOMATO TARRAGON SAUCE

4 skinless, boneless
   chicken breast halves
¼ cup all-purpose flour
Salt
Freshly ground black
   pepper
2 tablespoons butter
1 tablespoon vegetable oil
1 tablespoon brandy or
   whiskey
1 small onion, chopped
3 large garlic cloves,
   chopped

2 large ripe tomatoes
   (1 pound), seeded and
   diced
1 tablespoon dried tarragon
¼ cup dry white vermouth
¼ cup chicken stock
¾ cup heavy cream
Salt
Lots of freshly ground black
   pepper
2 tablespoons finely
   chopped fresh parsley

BETWEEN TWO PIECES of plastic wrap, pound chicken
breasts with smooth mallet or rolling pin to ¼-inch
thickness.

Combine flour, salt, and pepper on piece of wax paper.
Coat chicken with seasoned flour, shaking off excess.

Melt butter with oil in large nonstick skillet over
medium-high heat. Cook chicken for 4 minutes each side
or until golden brown and just cooked through; do not
overcook; remove to a plate.

Add brandy to skillet and cook for 2 seconds or until
deglazed. Add onion and garlic and a little butter if necessary; cook for 2 minutes or until tender. Stir in tomatoes
and tarragon and cook for 4 minutes or until soft. Add
vermouth, chicken stock, cream, salt, and pepper; turn heat
to high and bring to a boil. Cook for 4 minutes or until
thickened. Reduce heat to low, return chicken to sauce to
reheat. Transfer to warmed plates and sprinkle with parsley.
Serves 2 to 4.

TANDOORI CHICKEN

1 cup plain yogurt	1 teaspoon salt
¼ cup fresh lime juice	½ teaspoon ground cumin
2 tablespoons vegetable oil	½ teaspoon dry mustard
4 large garlic cloves, chopped	½ teaspoon cayenne
	½ teaspoon freshly ground black pepper
2 tablespoons finely chopped fresh ginger	¼ teaspoon turmeric
1 teaspoon curry powder	4 chicken breast halves

PREPARE GRILL or preheat broiler.

Combine yogurt, lime juice, oil, garlic, ginger, curry powder, salt, cumin, mustard, cayenne, pepper, and turmeric in bowl.

Arrange chicken side by side in a small nonreactive baking dish and pour marinade over. Cover and refrigerate several hours or overnight, turning occasionally.

Remove chicken from marinade and grill or broil for 8 minutes per side, basting with marinade, or until golden brown and cooked through. Serves 2 to 4.

The combination of yogurt, lime juice, and fragrant seasonings in this marinade creates succulent grilled chicken. I also like to use this marinade with chicken wings. ◆ Delicious served with Basmati Rice with Garlic and Ginger (page 91).

In this recipe, chicken is simply marinated in a lovely coconut-flavored marinade, then grilled and served with a delicate mango dipping sauce. ♦ This chicken is delicious accompanied by scented Thai rice (available at Asian grocery stores) and Glass Noodle Chicken Salad (page 71), substituting ground pork or veal for the chicken. ♦ Coconut milk (not the coconut cream used in mixed drinks!) is available in Asian and Caribbean food stores.

CHICKEN SATAY WITH CURRIED MANGO SAUCE

½ cup coconut milk
1 large garlic clove, chopped
3 tablespoons sugar
1 tablespoon best-quality curry powder
1 teaspoon salt
1 teaspoon turmeric
2 tablespoons soy sauce
2 tablespoons vegetable oil
1 teaspoon sambal oelek or hot red pepper flakes
6 skinless, boneless chicken breast halves, cut into 2 x ½-inch strips

2 perfectly ripe mangos, peeled, seeded, and puréed in food processor (1½ cups purée)
¼ cup mayonnaise
½ teaspoon best-quality curry powder
Salt
Freshly ground black pepper

COMBINE COCONUT MILK, garlic, sugar, curry powder, salt, turmeric, soy sauce, oil, and sambal oelek in large bowl. Add chicken and stir to coat evenly. Cover, and marinate in refrigerator for several hours or overnight. Bring to room temperature before grilling.

Prepare grill or preheat broiler.

To prepare Curried Mango Sauce, combine mango purée, mayonnaise, curry powder, salt, and pepper in small serving bowl. Cover and refrigerate if not using immediately.

Thread about 4 pieces of marinated chicken onto each of about ten 10-inch bamboo skewers. Wrap exposed parts of bamboo with foil to prevent them from burning.

Place skewers on lightly greased grill, or broiling rack with bottom pan and place under broiler. Grill satays for 10 minutes, turning once, or until lightly charred and cooked through but still moist inside. (Test center pieces for doneness: they take longest to cook.) Remove foil from skewers and serve at once with mango sauce. Serves 3 to 5.

coconut
milk

U nlikely as it may seem, chicken breasts brushed with mayonnaise and tarragon before they're broiled not only enhances their flavor but bestows a pretty grilled appearance on the chicken. ♦ A breeze to make, this has become a standby in my kitchen: I usually have boneless chicken breasts in the freezer, mayonnaise in the refrigerator, and tarragon in the spice cupboard. ♦ With this, I serve white or wild rice (see Index) or Halved Baked Potatoes (page 79), and a crisp salad of mixed greens. ♦ For maximum flavor, make sure your dried tarragon is aromatic and bright green.

CHICKEN BREASTS WITH TARRAGON MAYONNAISE GLAZE

¼ cup mayonnaise
2 tablespoons Dijon mustard
2 tablespoons fresh lemon juice
1 tablespoon dried tarragon
Salt
Freshly ground black pepper
4 skinless, boneless chicken breast halves

PREHEAT BROILER.

Thoroughly combine mayonnaise, mustard, lemon juice, tarragon, salt, and pepper in small bowl. Transfer half of the mixture to another small serving dish to serve at the table.

Between two pieces of plastic wrap, pound chicken breasts with smooth mallet or rolling pin to ¼-inch thickness.

Place chicken breasts on broiling rack with bottom pan; brush top of chicken with half of mayonnaise glaze mixture.

Broil for 4 minutes and turn, and brush with remaining glaze mixture and cook for 4 minutes or just until cooked through and speckled with golden brown; do not overcook. Serve with reserved sauce. Serves 2 to 4.

SESAME CHICKEN STRIPS WITH GARLIC MAYONNAISE

½ cup mayonnaise
1 small garlic clove, finely chopped
1 tablespoon fresh lemon juice
½ teaspoon dry mustard
Scant ½ cup all-purpose flour
Scant ½ cup sesame seeds

½ teaspoon cayenne
1 extra-large egg
2 tablespoons milk
4 skinless, boneless chicken breast halves, cut into ½-inch strips
¾ cup vegetable oil
Salt

COMBINE MAYONNAISE, garlic, lemon juice, and mustard in small serving bowl; set aside.

Combine flour, sesame seeds, and cayenne on large piece of wax paper. Whisk egg and milk in small wide bowl.

One at a time, dip chicken strips into egg mixture, allowing excess to drain off, then coat evenly with seasoned flour mixture.

Heat oil in large nonstick skillet over medium-high heat. Fry strips, in batches if necessary, for 3 minutes or until golden brown and cooked through; do not overcook. Remove to paper towel-lined plate to drain and sprinkle with a little salt. Serve with Garlic Mayonnaise. Serves 2 to 4.

A breeze to cook, this casual dish can be prepared ahead, covered and refrigerated, then fried just prior to serving. ◆ Serve with a salad of mixed vegetables.

A hearty, piquant taste of Mexico. Chopped fresh coriander would be a delicious addition to the garnish. ♦ The bean dip is also delicious served as a warm dip with tortilla chips.

MEXICAN CHICKEN

2 tablespoons olive oil
¼ cup finely chopped red onion
2 large garlic cloves, finely chopped
3 whole pickled jalapeños, chopped
1 large ripe tomato, chopped
1 tablespoon chopped fresh parsley
2 tablespoons fresh lemon juice

14-ounce can refried beans
½ teaspoon best-quality chili powder
4 chicken breast halves
2 cups (about 8 ounces) grated Monterey Jack or Cheddar cheese
4 whole green onions, chopped (garnish)
2 large ripe tomatoes, chopped (garnish)
Tortilla chips
Sour cream

HEAT OIL in medium saucepan over medium-high heat. Add onion, garlic, chiles, tomato, parsley, and lemon juice; cook, stirring, for 3 minutes. Add refried beans and chili powder; cook for 2 minutes.

In food processor, blend bean mixture in batches (do not overprocess: it should be smooth but with some texture) and return to pan. Reduce heat to medium; cook, stirring, for 4 minutes. Set aside; keep warm.

Place chicken in small roasting pan. Bake in 400°F oven for 30 minutes or just until cooked through.

While chicken is still warm, tear into thickstrips – discarding skin and bones – and place on broilerproof platter. Top with warm bean dip. Sprinkle cheese on top. Place platter under broiler for 2 minutes or until chicken is reheated and cheese melts. Remove and garnish with green onions and tomatoes. Place tortilla chips around edge of platter. Pass sour cream at the table. Serves 4 to 6.

jalapeños

A nother wonderfully quick and simple – and very tasty – chicken entrée. ◆ Serve with Orzo with Parmesan Cheese (page 86).

MUSTARD TARRAGON CHICKEN BREASTS

2 large garlic cloves, finely chopped
3 tablespoons Dijon mustard
3 tablespoons fresh lemon juice
2 teaspoons dried tarragon
4 boneless chicken breast halves, with skin on
Salt
Freshly ground black pepper

PREHEAT OVEN to 400°F.

Combine garlic, mustard, lemon juice, and tarragon in small bowl. Loosen skin from one side of each chicken breast; spoon about 2 teaspoons mustard mixture under skin of each. Spread remaining mixture equally over chicken, then salt and pepper lightly.

Place chicken skin side up in small baking dish and form them into mound shapes. Bake for 30 minutes, basting frequently with pan juices, or until cooked through and skin is crisp. Serves 2 to 4.

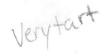
Very tart

CHICKEN BREASTS STUFFED WITH GOAT CHEESE AND SUN-DRIED TOMATOES

Grated zest of 1 medium orange
4 large sun-dried tomato halves in olive oil, drained
5 ounces mild soft goat cheese, at room temperature
¼ cup (2 ounces/½ stick) butter, at room temperature
½ teaspoon hot red pepper flakes
6 boneless chicken breast halves, with skin on
¼ cup pecan halves, finely chopped

PREHEAT OVEN to 400°F.

Place grated zest and sun-dried tomatoes in food processor and process until tomatoes are finely chopped. Add cheese, butter, and hot red pepper flakes; process until smooth.

Loosen skin from one side of each breast; spoon equal amounts of cheese mixture under skin, using all but 1 tablespoon of mixture. Tuck skin completely over filling, then form chicken into mound shapes. Place in small baking dish, spread remaining butter mixture over each one, and sprinkle with chopped pecans, patting to help them adhere. Bake for 30 minutes or just until cooked through. Serves 3 to 6.

*E*legant and easy, these dramatic and delicious chicken breasts are enhanced by a stuffing of tangy goat cheese and sun-dried tomatoes. ♦ As a variation, place a large fresh basil leaf directly on top of the stuffing mixture. ♦ Serve with a salad of mixed greens or Stir-Fried Zucchini (page 84). ♦ To finely chop the pecans, I place them in a plastic freezer or sandwich bag, then lightly crush with a rolling pin – a food processor tends to overprocess.

*J*ust a hint of mint and lemon flavors this appealing dish. ♦ Serve with steamed pencil-thin asparagus and crusty French bread.

MINTED LEMON CHICKEN BREASTS

¼ cup chopped fresh mint leaves
Finely grated zest of 1 small lemon
1 small garlic clove, finely chopped
4 chicken breast halves
Salt
Freshly ground black pepper
3 tablespoons fresh lemon juice
2 tablespoons vegetable oil

PREHEAT OVEN to 400°F.

Combine mint, lemon zest, and garlic in small bowl. Loosen skin from one side of each chicken breast; stuff equal portions of mixture under loosened skin of each, pressing edges down to keep stuffing in while baking. Sprinkle with salt and pepper. Arrange chicken skin side up in nonreactive baking dish just large enough to hold them in one layer.

Combine lemon juice and oil in small bowl and brush skin with a little of the mixture. Bake for 30 minutes, basting occasionally with lemon mixture, or until chicken is tender. Serves 4.

ROQUEFORT CHICKEN BREASTS

6 green onions (green part only), chopped
2 large garlic cloves, finely chopped
Freshly ground black pepper

Salt
6 chicken breast halves
6 ounces Roquefort cheese, at room temperature
2 tablespoons lightly toasted sesame seeds

PREHEAT OVEN to 400°F.

Combine green onions, garlic, pepper, and a little salt in small bowl. Loosen skin from one side of each chicken breast; spoon equal portions of mixture under loosened skin of each, pressing edges down to keep stuffing in while baking.

Place chicken skin side up in small baking dish. Bake for 30 minutes or until just cooked through. Remove from oven and carefully place about 1 ounce of cheese under skin of each breast; be careful: they're hot! Sprinkle sesame seeds over chicken and return to oven for 3 minutes to melt cheese. Serve at once. Serves 3 to 6.

A sumptuous chicken dish, the blue cheese tucked under the skin is rich and delicious. ◆ Serve with steamed green beans and sliced ripe tomatoes.

B athed in a potent orange-flavored sauce, this chicken dish couldn't be simpler. ◆ Serve with white or wild rice (pages 88, 89), of course, and steamed broccoli florets.

ORANGE CHICKEN

4 skinless, boneless
  chicken breast halves
¼ cup all-purpose flour
Salt
Freshly ground black
  pepper
3 tablespoons butter
3 large garlic cloves,
  chopped
1 small onion, chopped
1 teaspoon all-purpose
  flour

5 tablespoons thawed
  frozen orange juice
  concentrate
½ cup water
¼ cup dry white vermouth
1 tablespoon Cointreau
2 tablespoons chopped
  fresh parsley
Grated zest of 1 orange

BETWEEN TWO PIECES of plastic wrap, pound chicken breasts with smooth mallet or rolling pin to ¼-inch thickness.

Combine flour, salt, and pepper on piece of wax paper. Coat chicken with seasoned flour, shaking off excess.

Melt 2 tablespoons butter in large nonstick or nonreactive skillet over medium-high heat. Add chicken and cook for 4 minutes each side or until golden brown and just cooked through; remove to a plate.

Melt remaining butter; add garlic and onion and cook for 2 minutes or until tender. Stir in flour and cook for 1 minute. Add orange juice concentrate, water, vermouth, Cointreau, salt, and pepper; simmer for 2 minutes or until thickened. Reduce heat to low, return chicken to sauce to reheat, sprinkle with parsley and orange zest, and serve. Serves 2 to 4.

TERIYAKI CHICKEN

2 large garlic cloves, peeled and lightly smashed
1 quarter-size slice fresh ginger, lightly smashed
1 whole green onion, cut in half
¼ cup Japanese soy sauce
¼ cup dry sherry
2 tablespoons vegetable oil
1 tablespoon sesame oil
3 tablespoons liquid honey
½ teaspoon hot red pepper flakes
4 skinless, boneless chicken breast halves
1 tablespoon lightly toasted sesame seeds

COMBINE GARLIC, ginger, green onion, soy sauce, sherry, oil, sesame oil, honey, and red pepper flakes in nonreactive dish just large enough to hold chicken in one layer. Add chicken, turn several times to coat evenly, and marinate for 3 hours, covered, in refrigerator.

Meanwhile, prepare grill or preheat broiler.

Remove chicken from marinade and place on grill or broiling rack with bottom pan. Cook for 5 minutes each side or just until cooked through. Transfer to cutting surface, slice each chicken breast on the diagonal every inch or so. Transfer chicken to warmed plates, reforming chicken into original shape, and sprinkle with sesame seeds. Serves 4.

G rilled or broiled soy-marinated chicken is a quick and tasty dinner accompanied by White Rice (page 88) and steamed broccoli florets or stir-fried vegetables.

Quickly prepared, this tasty dish features warmed Mexican flour tortillas wrapped around Middle-Eastern-flavored chick-pea dip, sautéed chicken strips, fresh cherry tomatoes, and shredded lettuce. ◆ The dip is quickly made in a food processor and can be made ahead of time and chilled if you wish. (Bring dip back to room temperature before serving.) ◆ In place of tortillas you can use pitas.

CHICKEN CHICK-PEA ROLL-UPS

6 flour tortillas (8 inches in diameter)
½ small red onion
2 garlic cloves
¼ cup fresh parsley
¼ cup olive or vegetable oil
19-ounce can chick-peas, drained
2 tablespoons fresh lemon juice
1 tablespoon mayonnaise
½ teaspoon salt

Freshly ground black pepper
3 skinless, boneless chicken breast halves, cut into ½-inch strips
2 tablespoons all-purpose flour
2 tablespoons vegetable oil
1 tablespoon butter
Diced ripe cherry tomatoes
Shredded Romaine lettuce leaves

cherry tomatoes

SPRINKLE TORTILLAS with a little water, wrap completely in foil, and place in 250°F oven to warm while preparing remaining ingredients.

Chop onion in food processor (you should have ¼ cup). Add garlic and parsley and chop. Add oil, chick-peas, lemon juice, mayonnaise, salt, and pepper and process until combined but do not overblend; it should be smooth, but still have some texture.

Transfer to a serving bowl.

Toss chicken strips with flour and a little salt and pepper. Heat oil and butter in medium nonstick skillet over medium-high heat. Add chicken and cook for 5 minutes or until golden brown and just cooked through.

Place tomatoes and lettuce in separate bowls.

To eat, each person takes a tortilla, spoons about ¼ cup chick-pea dip in center, tops with some chicken, tomatoes, and lettuce, then rolls it up and eats it like a sandwich. Serves 3 to 6.

T ender chicken breasts swathed in a creamy mushroom and tarragon sauce are as delicious as they are easy to prepare. ◆ Serve with buttered egg noodles or Wild Rice (page 89) and steamed baby carrots.

CHICKEN BREASTS IN CREAMY MUSHROOM SAUCE

4 skinless, boneless
   chicken breast halves
¼ cup all-purpose flour
Salt
Freshly ground black
   pepper
4 tablespoons butter
1 small onion, chopped
8 medium-large
   mushrooms, coarsely
   chopped

½ cup chicken stock
¼ cup dry white vermouth
¾ cup heavy cream
½ teaspoon dried tarragon
¼ teaspoon salt
Freshly ground black
   pepper

BETWEEN TWO PIECES of plastic wrap, pound chicken breasts with smooth mallet or rolling pin to ¼-inch thickness.

Combine flour, salt, and pepper on piece of wax paper. Coat chicken with seasoned flour, shaking off excess.

Melt 2 tablespoons butter in large nonstick skillet over medium-high heat. Add chicken and cook for 4 minutes each side or until golden and just cooked through; remove to a plate.

Melt remaining butter; add onion and mushrooms and cook for 2 minutes or until tender. Add chicken stock and vermouth and cook for 4 minutes or until slightly reduced. Add heavy cream, tarragon, salt, and pepper and simmer another 4 minutes or until thickened. Reduce heat to low, return chicken to sauce to reheat, and serve immediately. Serves 2 to 4.

CHICKEN FINGERS WITH DILL DIP

¼ cup (2 ounces) cream
   cheese, at room
   temperature
¼ cup mayonnaise
¼ cup sour cream
1 green onion (green part
   only), finely chopped
1 tablespoon chopped fresh
   dill
Freshly ground black
   pepper
About ½ cup all-purpose
   flour

2 teaspoons Lawry's
   Seasoned Salt
Lots of freshly ground black
   pepper
¼ to ½ teaspoon cayenne
About 1½ cups fine dry
   bread crumbs
2 large eggs
6 boneless, skinless
   chicken breast halves, cut
   into ½-inch strips
1 cup vegetable oil

PREHEAT OVEN to 400°F.

To prepare dip, combine cream cheese, mayonnaise, sour cream, green onion, dill, and pepper in small serving bowl.

Combine flour, seasoned salt, pepper, and cayenne on large piece of wax paper. Place bread crumbs on another large piece of wax paper. Beat eggs in small bowl.

Dip chicken strips into seasoned flour, shaking off excess, then into beaten eggs, allowing excess to drain. Coat strips in bread crumbs.

Heat oil in large nonstick skillet over medium-high heat. Fry strips, in batches, for 1 minute or just until light golden. Using tongs, transfer to baking sheet and bake for 8 minutes or just until cooked through; do not overcook. Serve at once with Dill Dip. Serves 4 to 6.

*S*trips of chicken are first quickly fried, then baked, which ensures a crispy coating and marvelously tender chicken. ◆ A bowl of refreshing Dill Dip and perhaps Spicy Okra Stew (page 80), or Spinach, Mushroom, and Sweet Onion Salad (page 83), perfectly complete this simple meal.

The French call this robust salad-in-a-sandwich Pan Bagnat, which means <u>pain</u> <u>baigné</u> or "bathed bread." ♦ *I like to serve these sandwiches at casual summer gatherings. They are so simple to mass produce: just set out the ingredients and make them to order. You must have good-quality, round crusty sandwich rolls, or bread slices from a large French baguette, or pita bread that's been split in half so you have two full circles. Soft, fluffy bread or rolls just won't do.* ♦ *The following toppings are for one sandwich; just increase the amounts according to the number of servings required.*

DELUXE CHICKEN SANDWICH

1 round crusty roll, about 5 inches in diameter
Small handful watercress leaves
2 slices ripe tomato
A few paper-thin slices ham
A few pieces cooked chicken
1 thinly sliced ring sweet red pepper
A few slices marinated artichokes
A few pitted, sliced black olives, (Kalamata)
Capers (optional)
Finely chopped garlic (optional)
Thinly sliced red onion rings (optional)
Anchovies (optional)
Soft mild goat cheese
⅓ cup olive oil
2 tablespoons red wine vinegar, or to taste
Chopped fresh or dried basil
Dried thyme
Salt
Freshly ground black pepper

CUT CRUSTY ROLL in half and scoop out the inside, leaving ½-inch shell.

Place watercress, tomato, ham, chicken, red pepper, artichokes, olives, and any of the optional ingredients, on bottom half of roll in order given. Spread top half with goat cheese and set aside. Whisk oil, vinegar, a little basil, and thyme in small bowl; drizzle over filling, then sprinkle over a little salt and pepper. You can close the sandwich or do what I do: set the two halves side by side on plate to show off pretty filling. Traditionally, the top is placed on and pressed down, then the whole thing wrapped tightly, and enjoyed several hours later after the flavors have married. Serves 1.

oil & vinegar

A very easily made dish, the chicken is sautéed in butter, mustard, and herbs with a savory coating of Parmesan cheese. ◆ Serve with Green Beans with Peppers and Tomatoes (page 76) or a crisp salad, and crusty Italian bread.

PARMESAN CHICKEN BREASTS

4 skinless, boneless
    chicken breast halves
¼ cup (2 ounces/½ stick)
    butter
2 teaspoons Dijon mustard
1 garlic clove, finely
    chopped
1 teaspoon fresh lemon
    juice

¼ teaspoon salt
¼ teaspoon freshly ground
    black pepper
¼ teaspoon dried oregano
¼ cup freshly grated
    Parmesan cheese
2 tablespoons fine dry
    bread crumbs

BETWEEN TWO PIECES of plastic wrap, pound chicken breasts with smooth mallet or rolling pin to ¼-inch thickness.

Melt butter in large nonstick skillet over medium heat. Add mustard, garlic, lemon juice, salt, pepper, and oregano and cook for 1 minute. Add chicken and cook for 4 minutes each side or until golden brown and just cooked through.

Reduce heat to low, sprinkle cheese and bread crumbs over chicken and turn a few times to coat evenly. Transfer to warmed plates and serve at once. Serves 2 to 4.

CHICKEN IN CREAMY MUSTARD SAUCE

4 to 6 skinless, boneless
   chicken breast halves
¼ cup all-purpose flour
Salt
Freshly ground black
   pepper
3 tablespoons butter
2 large garlic cloves,
   chopped

1 small onion, chopped
¼ cup dry white vermouth
¼ cup coarse-grained
   mustard
¼ cup Dijon mustard
1 cup heavy cream
1 teaspoon dried tarragon

BETWEEN TWO PIECES of plastic wrap, pound chicken breasts with smooth mallet or rolling pin to ¼-inch thickness.

Combine flour, salt, and pepper on piece of wax paper. Coat chicken with seasoned flour, shaking off excess.

Melt butter in large nonstick skillet over medium-high heat. Add chicken and cook for 4 minutes each side or until golden brown and just cooked through; remove to a plate.

Add garlic and onion and cook for 2 minutes or until tender. Add vermouth and cook for 1 minute or until reduced by half. Whisk in mustards, cream, and tarragon, blending well; simmer for 4 minutes or until thickened. Reduce heat to low, return chicken to sauce to reheat, and serve at once. Serves 4 to 6.

*T*he combination of coarse-grained and Dijon mustards in a creamy tarragon sauce makes very piquant chicken.
♦ *Wild Rice (page 89) and a tossed green salad are particularly good with this. Or serve with buttered egg noodles and tiny green peas.*

LEGS, THIGHS, & WINGS

♦ ♦ ♦

When I wrote my book, _The Complete Book of Chicken Wings_, seven years ago, everyone exclaimed "a whole book on chicken wings?!" Happily, I'm still discovering more and more delicious recipes for the tastiest part of the bird. ♦ This recipe was contributed by Vicky Fabbri. Serve with a baked potato and a crisp green salad.

SPICY TARRAGON WINGS

4 pounds chicken wings
3 tablespoons dried
   tarragon
1 tablespoon Lawry's
   Seasoned Salt

2 teaspoons garlic powder
Freshly ground black
   pepper

PREHEAT OVEN to 450°F.

Trim wings: cut off wing tips and save for stock or discard. Cut away "triangle" of skin between the two sections, then cut each wing into two parts.

Thoroughly mix tarragon, seasoned salt, garlic powder, and pepper in large bowl. Toss wings in mixture until evenly coated. Arrange wings skin side up in single layer on lightly greased rack set over baking sheet, or on broiling rack with bottom pan. Bake for 30 minutes, without turning, or until skin is crisp. Serves 4.

CHILI CHICKEN WINGS

2½ pounds chicken wings
1 tablespoon garlic powder
2 teaspoons best-quality
   chili powder
2 teaspoons paprika

1 teaspoon cayenne
1 teaspoon salt
½ teaspoon freshly ground
   black pepper

PREHEAT OVEN to 450°F.

Trim wings: cut off wing tips and save for stock or discard. Cut away "triangle" of skin between the two sections, then cut each wing into two parts.

Thoroughly blend garlic powder, chili powder, paprika, cayenne, salt, and pepper in large bowl. Toss wings in mixture until evenly coated. Arrange wings skin side up in single layer on lightly greased rack set over baking sheet, or on broiling rack with bottom pan. Bake for 30 minutes, without turning, or until skin is crisp. Serves 2.

Yummy, hot and spicy wings are easy to make and sure to please wing aficionados. ◆ Serve with a refreshingly crisp green salad and Halved Baked Potatoes (page 79) or baked potatoes.

E veryone's favorite Italian
chicken entrée. I think you'll
enjoy this particularly robust
rendition especially if made
ahead: it tastes even better reheated. ♦
Delicious with buttered egg noodles,
Stir-Fried Zucchini (page 84), and crusty
Italian bread – or with rice and steamed
green beans. ♦ Traditionally prepared
with a whole cut-up chicken, I prefer
chicken thighs because they take so well
to braising.

CHICKEN CACCIATORA

½ cup all-purpose flour
Salt
Freshly ground black
  pepper
3 pounds chicken thighs
3 tablespoons olive oil
1 large onion, thinly sliced
4 large garlic cloves,
  chopped
1 large sweet red pepper,
  cut into julienne

¼ cup dry white vermouth
¼ cup chicken stock
14-ounce can Italian plum
  tomatoes, undrained
1 tablespoon dried basil
1 large bay leaf
¼ teaspoon hot red pepper
  flakes
½ teaspoon salt
½ teaspoon freshly ground
  black pepper

COMBINE FLOUR, salt, and pepper on large piece of wax paper. Coat chicken with seasoned flour, shaking off excess.

Heat oil in large nonstick skillet or heavy Dutch oven over medium-high heat. Brown chicken in batches and remove to a plate. Pour off all but 2 tablespoons oil. Reduce heat to medium-low, add onion and garlic and cook for 2 minutes or until tender. Add red pepper and cook for 2 minutes or just until tender. Add vermouth and chicken stock, turn heat to high, and cook until liquid is slightly reduced, about 3 minutes.

Return chicken to skillet and add tomatoes including liquid – crushing them as you add them – then basil, bay leaf, hot red pepper flakes, salt, and pepper. Reduce heat to low, cover, and cook for 45 minutes or until chicken is very tender, turning and stirring frequently.

Transfer chicken to warm platter. Skim off surface fat, if any, and if sauce is thin, turn heat to high and cook until thickened. Spoon over chicken. Serves 4 to 5.

sweet red pepper

On our drive to Florida each winter, Drew and I taste our way through New York State, Pennsylvania, Maryland, the Carolinas, and Georgia. We feast on spiedies (grilled chunks of lamb or pork) from Drew's home town of Binghamton, New York; hearty Amish soups and pies; steamed blue crabs; barbecue; and Southern-fried chicken. ◆ A favorite eatery of ours in South Carolina has an incredible all-you-can-eat fried-chicken buffet. I copy their style and serve rice with chicken gravy and collards, or Spinach, Mushroom, and Sweet Onion Salad (page 83).

CLASSIC FRIED CHICKEN

⅔ cup buttermilk
1 large egg
A few dashes Tabasco
1 cup all-purpose flour
1 teaspoon salt
1 teaspoon freshly ground
black pepper

6 chicken pieces – thighs or
legs, and breasts
1 pound lard or vegetable
shortening
½ cup vegetable oil

PREHEAT OVEN to 375°F.

Whisk buttermilk, egg, and Tabasco in medium bowl. Combine flour, salt, and pepper on large piece of wax paper. Dip chicken into buttermilk mixture, then coat in seasoned flour.

Heat lard or vegetable shortening and oil in large high-sided heavy skillet or deep fryer to 340°F. Fry chicken for 8 minutes or just until golden brown. Using tongs, transfer chicken to rack in baking dish and bake for 20 minutes or until cooked through. Serves 3 to 6.

SOY-BRAISED CHICKEN THIGHS

3 dried Chinese
  mushrooms,
  reconstituted in hot
  water for 30 minutes
1-inch cinnamon stick
4 thick quarter-size slices
  unpeeled ginger
4 to 6 large garlic cloves,
  peeled and left whole
1 star anise
2½ cups chicken stock

½ cup soy sauce
¼ cup dry sherry (optional)
2 tablespoons brown sugar
1 teaspoon salt
8 skinless chicken thighs
10 fresh water chestnuts,
  peeled
10-ounce can sliced
  bamboo shoots, drained
1 teaspoon sesame oil

BRING FIRST TEN ingredients to a boil in large saucepan; add chicken. Reduce heat to low, cover, and cook, turning chicken frequently, for 1 hour or until chicken is very tender.

Add water chestnuts and bamboo shoots and cook for 5 minutes. Drizzle in sesame oil. To serve, transfer chicken with a slotted spoon to a warmed platter and spoon some of the braising liquid over.

Leftover braising liquid can be frozen (remove cinnamon and star anise) and used again; simply replenish some of the liquid and seasonings. Serves 4 to 8.

I have a passion for Chinese food. ♦ This super-easy pungent Chinese casserole is easily put together and can be done ahead, too. ♦ The perfect accompaniment is White Rice (page 88), or Basmati Rice with Garlic and Ginger (page 91); or boiled, peeled potato halves. You might wish to add a stir-fried vegetable such as snow peas, thinly sliced onion rings, bean sprouts, and julienned sweet red pepper.

Simple and savory, chicken thighs become tangy and meltingly tender braised in this happy marriage of garlic and lemon. The garlic mellows sweetly in the sauce so don't reduce the amount. And don't add another lemon either – I've already tried it with mouth-puckering results! ◆ White Rice (page 88) is the perfect accompaniment.

BRAISED LEMONY CHICKEN THIGHS

2 tablespoons butter	1 medium lemon, peeled, thinly sliced and seeded
6 chicken thighs	½ cup chicken stock
20 large garlic cloves (1 whole head), peeled and left whole	½ cup dry white vermouth
2 tablespoons all-purpose flour	Salt
	Freshly ground black pepper

MELT BUTTER in large nonstick skillet over medium-high heat. Brown chicken, about 4 minutes; remove to a plate.

Remove all but 2 tablespoons oil; add garlic and cook for 2 minutes. Remove from heat, stir in flour, then return to heat. Cook, stirring constantly, for 2 minutes. Add lemon, chicken stock, vermouth, salt, and pepper; bring to a boil, stirring constantly. Return chicken, cover, and reduce heat to medium-low. Simmer for 45 minutes or until thighs are very tender. Serves 4 to 6.

CHILE-RUBBED CHICKEN

3.5-ounce can pickled
  sliced jalapeños,
  undrained
8 skinless chicken thighs
¾ cup yellow cornmeal
2 tablespoons best-quality
  chili powder

1 teaspoon cayenne
1 teaspoon salt
¼ cup (2 ounces/½ stick)
  butter

PREHEAT OVEN to 400°F.

Purée chiles and liquid in food processor until smooth. Generously brush on chicken. Combine cornmeal, chili powder, cayenne, and salt on large piece of wax paper. Coat chicken in cornmeal mixture, then place chicken on rack in baking dish. Melt butter and drizzle over chicken. Bake for 40 minutes or until tender. Serves 4 to 8.

*C*hiles give incredible flavor and, of course, heat while the cornmeal delivers a delicious crunchiness. ◆ Enjoy with Corn, Tomato, and Chile Salsa (page 87) and baked potatoes with sour cream.

nfused with the flavors of the Caribbean, this chicken is meltingly tender with a taste that is too good to be true!

I devised this after sampling a similar version at a Caribbean restaurant and now it's one of my personal favorites. An effortless dish to make, it tastes even better prepared several hours or a day ahead and reheated. ♦ Caribbean hot sauce – searingly hot – is essential to this dish and is available in Caribbean food shops. A tiny amount is added to the sauce plus extra is served on the side for added zest and heat. ♦ Coconut milk (not the coconut cream used in mixed drinks!), is also required, and is available in Asian and Caribbean food stores. ♦ Serve with Basmati Rice with Ginger and Garlic (page 91), and Fried Plantains (page 85).

CARIBBEAN CURRIED CHICKEN

2 tablespoons vegetable oil
12 skinless chicken thighs
4 large garlic cloves, chopped
1 large onion, finely chopped
3 tablespoons all-purpose flour
5 tablespoons best-quality curry powder

1⅓ cups chicken stock
14-ounce can coconut milk
1 teaspoon salt
½ teaspoon allspice
¼ teaspoon freshly ground black pepper
1 bay leaf
1 teaspoon bottled Caribbean hot sauce plus extra for serving

HEAT OIL in large nonstick skillet over medium-high heat. Brown chicken in batches and remove to a plate.

Remove all but 3 tablespoons oil from skillet. Add garlic and onion and cook for 2 minutes or until tender. Stir in flour and curry powder and cook for 3 minutes, adding a little more oil if mixture is dry.

Pour in stock and bring to a boil, stirring constantly. Stir in coconut milk, salt, allspice, pepper, bay leaf, and hot sauce. Return chicken to skillet and bring to a boil. Reduce heat to low, cover, and simmer for 1 to 1½ hours, or until chicken is falling-off-the-bone tender, turning frequently. Remove pan from heat to cool a little, then skim off surface fat, if any. Transfer chicken and sauce to a warmed platter and serve bottled Caribbean hot sauce on the side. Serves 6 to 12.

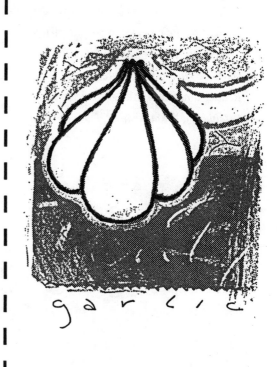

garlic

F*un-looking drumsticks covered in chopped peanuts make wonderfully messy finger food, so provide plenty of napkins.* ◆ *Serve with White Rice (page 88) and a simple green salad. Reduce amount of chili sauce if serving to children, if you wish.*

PEANUTTY DRUMSTICKS

1 small onion, quartered
1 large garlic clove
2 tablespoons butter, at room temperature
6 tablespoons creamy peanut butter
5 tablespoons soy sauce
3 tablespoon dry white vermouth
1 tablespoon fresh lemon juice
2 tablespoons Asian chili sauce (Yeo's brand)
3 tablespoons liquid honey
8 chicken drumsticks
½ cup peanuts, chopped

CHOP ONION and garlic in food processor. Add butter, peanut butter, soy sauce, vermouth, lemon juice, chili sauce, and honey and process until combined. Pour mixture into a nonreactive shallow pan just large enough to fit drumsticks. Roll drumsticks in marinade to coat well and marinate for 2 hours, covered, in refrigerator.

Preheat oven to 375°F.

Place chopped peanuts on large piece of wax paper. Roll one side of drumsticks in nuts until well coated. Place drumsticks peanut side up in clean baking dish and cover with aluminum foil. Bake for 40 minutes or until cooked through, uncovering pan for last 15 minutes. Serves 4 to 6.

CHICKEN PUTTANESCA

2 tablespoons olive oil	12 black olives (Kalamata),
8 chicken thighs	pitted and chopped
6 large garlic cloves,	2 tablespoons capers,
chopped	drained
28-ounce can Italian plum	½ cup chopped parsley,
tomatoes, undrained	plus extra for garnish
2 teaspoons dried oregano	Freshly grated Parmesan
½ teaspoon hot red pepper	cheese
flakes	

PREHEAT OVEN to 375°F.

Heat oil in large nonstick skillet over medium-high heat. Add chicken and brown in batches, removing to nonreactive baking dish just large enough to hold chicken; set aside.

Spoon off all but 1 tablespoon oil; add garlic and cook for 1 minute. Add tomatoes, including liquid, oregano, and hot red pepper flakes; cook for 20 minutes or until sauce is slightly thickened. Stir in olives, capers, and parsley. Pour sauce over chicken and bake, uncovered, for 30 minutes or until tender. Sprinkle with chopped parsley and Parmesan cheese just before serving. Serves 4 to 8.

B y now some of you know my passion for garlic, capers, olives, and red pepper flakes, especially when combined to produce that wonderful, spicy Italian pasta sauce. I've included it in two of my All the Best books on pasta and pizza and have happily discovered that its robust flavor is absolutely superb with chicken, too. ♦ Serve atop cooked buttered pasta, such as wide egg noodles, with Spinach, Mushroom, and Sweet Onion Salad (page 83), and a full-bodied red wine.

My version of the classic Moroccan chicken stew is wonderfully assertive with the flavors of lemon and olives. ◆ The black olives are unpitted, by the way, so do alert your dinner companions. Though not authentic, I use pimiento-stuffed green olives in place of unpitted green olives. ◆ The perfect accompaniment: Couscous (page 92).

CHICKEN WITH GREEN AND BLACK OLIVES

2 tablespoons olive oil
6 chicken pieces – thighs or legs, and breasts
5 large garlic cloves, chopped
1 large onion, chopped
1 tablespoon all-purpose flour
2 teaspoons ground ginger
1 teaspoon paprika
½ teaspoon turmeric
¼ teaspoon cayenne

1 medium lemon, unpeeled, thinly sliced, and seeded
2 cups chicken stock
½ teaspoon salt
1 cup black olives (Kalamata)
1 cup pimiento-stuffed green olives
Fresh coriander leaves (garnish)

HEAT OIL in large nonstick or nonreactive skillet over medium-high heat. Brown chicken in batches and remove to a plate.

Remove all but 2 tablespoons oil; add garlic and onion and cook for 2 minutes or until tender. Stir in flour, ginger, paprika, turmeric, and cayenne and cook for 2 minutes, stirring constantly. Return chicken; add lemon, chicken stock, and salt and bring to a boil. Cover, reduce heat to low, and simmer for 45 minutes or until chicken is tender. Transfer chicken to a plate with slotted spoon. Turn heat to high, bring sauce to a boil, and cook until slightly thickened, about 8 minutes. Reduce heat to low and skim off most of any surface fat. Return chicken and add olives to sauce to heat through. Garnish with coriander leaves and serve. Serves 4.

WHOLE & CUT-UP

CHICKEN

♦ ♦ ♦

Soul-satisfying chicken stew is one of my favorite meals for a nippy winter's eve. ◆ Dumplings cooked atop the bubbling stew make this sustaining food. The dumplings are variable: make herb dumplings by adding a little of your favorite chopped fresh or dried herbs such as thyme, parsley, basil, sage, or chives; or make whole wheat dumplings by substituting half the flour with whole wheat flour.

CHICKEN STEW WITH DUMPLINGS

2 tablespoons butter
2 tablespoons vegetable oil
3½-pound roasting chicken, cut up and skin removed
1 large onion, chopped
2 celery stalks, thinly sliced
4 medium carrots, cut into ½-inch pieces
¼ cup all-purpose flour plus 1 tablespoon
1 cup milk
6 cups chicken stock
½ teaspoon salt

½ teaspoon freshly ground black pepper
1 tablespoon dried thyme
1 bay leaf
3 whole cloves
¼ cup chopped fresh parsley
1 cup all-purpose flour
1 tablespoon baking powder
½ teaspoon salt
1 large egg, lightly beaten
½ cup milk

MELT BUTTER with oil in heavy Dutch oven over medium-high heat. Brown chicken in batches and remove to a plate.

Add onion, celery, and carrots and cook for 3 minutes or until onion is tender. Remove pan from heat; stir in flour. Return to heat, and cook vegetable roux for 5 minutes, stirring constantly, or until golden brown.

Remove pan from heat; stir in milk, chicken stock, salt, pepper, thyme, bay leaf, cloves, and parsley. Return to heat and bring to a boil, stirring constantly. Add chicken and reduce heat. simmer, partially covered, for 45 minutes. Using slotted spoon, remove chicken to a plate to cool enough to handle and remove and discard bay leaf and cloves.

Meanwhile, turn heat to high and cook stock until slightly thickened. Tear chicken into large bite-size pieces, discarding skin and bones; return to stew. Taste and adjust seasoning if necessary.

To make dumplings, combine flour, baking powder, salt, egg, and milk just until blended; do not overmix. Drop batter by tablespoonfuls on top of bubbling stock. Reduce heat to low, cover, and cook for 20 minutes – without peeking. Serves 4 to 6.

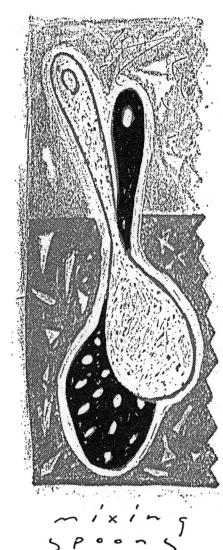

mixing spoons

A substantial, heartwarming dish that makes good cold-weather eating. ◆ My trick is to roast the chicken and prepare my pastry a day ahead (or use frozen puff pastry). Then, of course, it is a simple matter to prepare the pie the next day. The finished pie tastes even better prepared ahead and reheated. You can also make individual pies, remembering to reduce baking time. ◆ This is particulary good served with a crisp salad, and buttered crunchy seven-grain bread sticks.

CHICKEN POT PIE

5 tablespoons butter
½ pound mushrooms, sliced
2 large onions (1 pound), chopped
2 cups sliced carrots (about ¼ inch thick)
1½ cups diced celery
1 teaspoon salt
½ teaspoon freshly ground black pepper
1 tablespoon dried tarragon
4 tablespoons all-purpose flour
½ cup dry white vermouth
1½ cups chicken stock
½ cup heavy cream
Two 2½-pound chickens, roasted, skinned, boned, and meat torn into large bite-size pieces (about 5½ cups meat)
1 prepared pastry crust or puff pastry to fit 8 x 12-inch baking dish
1 egg white, beaten with 1 tablespoon water

MELT 2 TABLESPOONS butter in large nonstick skillet over high heat. Brown mushrooms quickly, about 2 minutes; remove to a plate. Add 3 tablespoons butter; add onions, carrots, celery and sauté until vegetables begin to soften, about 8 minutes; reducing heat if necessary. Remove from heat; add salt, pepper, tarragon, and flour, stirring well to coat vegetable mixture. Return to heat, and cook mixture for 4 minutes, stirring and scraping bits from bottom of skillet. Remove pan from heat; add vermouth, chicken stock, and cream and return to heat. Simmer, stirring, until thickened. Stir in mushrooms and cooked chicken. Pour into 8 x 12-inch baking dish and allow to cool completely. Cover with prepared pastry; brush with egg wash. Bake in preheated 400°F oven for 45 minutes or until pastry is golden and pie is bubbling. Serves 8.

creamer

*S*crumptious peppery and piquant chicken halves are grilled or broiled. You'll need a heavy cleaver or knife to split a whole chicken in half or ask your butcher to do it for you. ◆ Serve with Green Beans with Peppers and Tomatoes (page 76).

LEMON GARLIC PEPPER CHICKEN

3½-pound roasting
  chicken, split in half
⅔ cup fresh lemon juice
⅓ cup olive oil
4 large garlic cloves,
  chopped

1 tablespoon very coarsely
  ground (cracked) pepper
2 teaspoons salt

PLACE CHICKEN HALVES in nonreactive baking dish just large enough to hold them in one layer. Pour lemon juice over chicken halves, then drizzle over olive oil. Sprinkle with garlic, pepper, and salt, then turn the chicken several times to coat evenly with marinade. Set aside for a minimum of 2 hours to marinate, occasionally basting and turning chicken.

Prepare grill or preheat broiler.

Place chicken halves skin side up on grill or broiling rack with bottom pan. Cook, turning every 10 minutes, and basting with marinade, for 35 minutes or until cooked through. Serves 2 to 4.

CHICKEN RAGOUT WITH GARLIC AND TOMATO

3 tablespoons vegetable oil
Two 2-½ pound chickens,
  quartered
20 large garlic cloves
  (1 whole head), peeled
  and left whole
28-ounce can Italian plum
  tomatoes, drained
1 teaspoon dried thyme
⅛ teaspoon allspice
Several fennel seeds
1 bay leaf
1 cup chicken stock
½ cup dry white vermouth
Salt
Freshly ground black
  pepper
½ cup chopped fresh
  parsley plus extra
  for garnish

HEAT OIL in large nonstick skillet or heavy Dutch oven over medium-high heat. Brown chicken, then add garlic and cook for 1 minute. Add remaining ingredients and bring to a boil. Reduce heat to medium-low, cover, and simmer for 45 minutes or until chicken is very tender. Remove chicken with slotted spoon to a plate. Bring liquid to a boil on high heat and cook for 3 minutes or until slightly thickened. Return chicken to sauce to reheat. Transfer to warmed platter and garnish with parsley. Serves 6.

Intensely flavored, this chicken stew, like most, is best made ahead, then reheated. ◆ Serve with angel hair pasta, egg noodles, or rice and a green vegetable of your choice.

Heartily warming, this irresistible soup is perfect for a casual family dinner. ◆ I like to prepare it several hours or a day ahead, then all I need to do is make fresh homemade muffins (see recipes in my book, _All the Best Muffins and Quick Breads_), or serve good, store-bought rye bread.

HEARTY CHICKEN NOODLE SOUP

3-pound roasting chicken
3 quarts chicken stock
1 quart water
1 tablespoon black peppercorns
2 bay leaves
1 large onion, quartered with skin left on
1 stalk celery, cut in 3
1 medium carrot, cut in 3
1 bunch parsley stems, reserving leaves for later use*
3 thick quarter-size slices unpeeled fresh ginger
1 large onion, chopped
3 carrots coarsely diced

2 stalks celery, thinly sliced
2 cups sliced mushrooms (about 4 ounces)
1 cup finely chopped fresh parsley*
Salt
Freshly ground black pepper
1 heaping teaspoon dried chervil
1 heaping teaspoon dried thyme
12 ounces skinny egg noodles or angel hair pasta
4 whole green onions, finely chopped

PLACE CHICKEN, chicken stock, water, peppercorns, bay leaves, onion, celery, carrot, parsley stems, and ginger in large saucepan over high heat. Bring to a boil, then reduce heat to medium-low and simmer, partially covered, for 1 hour. Let chicken cool in stock for 1 hour. Remove chicken to large bowl and when cool enough to handle, pull chicken off bones into large bite-size pieces, discarding skin and bones. Strain stock through sieve, discarding solids. Return stock to saucepan and add cooked chicken, onion, carrots, celery, mushrooms, parsley, salt, pepper, chervil, and thyme. Simmer for 40 minutes or until vegetables are tender.

Cook pasta in large pot of boiling water until al dente. Drain noodles and stir into soup. Heat through, adjust seasonings, sprinkle with green onions and serve. Serves 8.

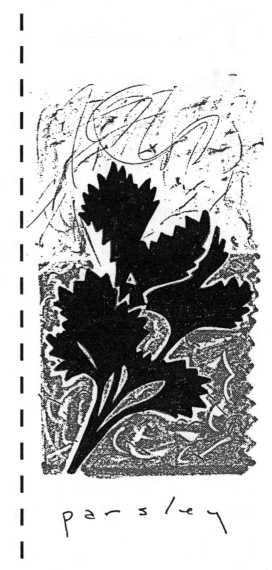

parsley

Everybody knows how to roast a chicken, don't they? Well, not everyone it seems. Sometimes it's the elementary things that are the most difficult to get just right. The secret is simple: the absolutely freshest (never frozen!) prime-quality chicken is cooked at high heat just until cooked through and still moist and juicy. ♦ Serve with almost any vegetables or grains (see Index). Some suggestions: Three-Grain Pilaf, Couscous, Sweet Potato Fries, Stir-Fried Zucchini, Green Beans with Coarse-Grained Mustard, mashed potatoes, Spinach, Mushroom, and Sweet Onion Salad, or Spicy Okra Tomato Stew.

PERFECT ROAST CHICKEN

4-pound roasting chicken
1 lemon, cut in half, then
    one half cut in wedges
1 small onion, cut into
    wedges
A few sprigs fresh thyme
Salt
Freshly ground black
    pepper
Dried thyme

PREHEAT OVEN to 425°F.

Place chicken in small roasting pan, breast side up. Squeeze juice of half lemon over bird, inside and out, then rub the skin with the squeezed half. Stuff cavity with remaining wedges of lemon, onion, and thyme sprigs. Tie legs together with kitchen string. Sprinkle with salt, pepper, and a little dried thyme.

Bake for 1 hour or until skin is golden brown and thigh juices run clear. Discard lemon, onion, and thyme from inside bird after carving. Serves 2 to 4.

CHICKEN

◆ ◆ ◆

C hicken burgers are an especially delicious alternative
to beef burgers. ◆ I like to
serve them as I've described
here, but you may serve them in ham-
burger buns or in pita bread with the red
pepper mayonnaise or with your own
favorite fixings. ◆ Ground chicken is now
available at most supermarkets and
butcher shops.

CHICKEN BURGERS WITH RED PEPPER MAYONNAISE

1 pound ground chicken
4 green onions (green part
  only), chopped
1/3 cup chopped fresh
  parsley
1/3 cup fine dry bread
  crumbs
2 1/2 tablespoons finely
  diced sweet red pepper
1 large egg
1/2 teaspoon salt
1/2 teaspoon freshly ground
  black pepper

1 large sweet red pepper
1/2 cup mayonnaise
2 tablespoons butter or
  vegetable oil
1 large ripe tomato or
  several cherry tomatoes,
  seeded and diced
  (garnish)
Italian flat-leaf parsley
  (garnish)

COMBINE CHICKEN, green onions, parsley, bread crumbs, red pepper, egg, salt, and pepper in medium bowl. Form into 4 to 6 equal-size patties; set aside.

To prepare red pepper mayonnaise, place whole pepper on piece of foil, broil until blackened and blistered on all sides. Remove from oven, wrap in foil, and set aside for 20 minutes. Remove foil, peel off blackened skin, and remove seeds and membrane. Pat dry with paper towels. Put pepper and mayonnaise in food processor and purée. Transfer to small serving bowl.

Heat butter or oil in large nonstick skillet over medium heat. Add patties and cook for 15 minutes, turning once or twice, or until cooked through. Transfer to warmed plates and garnish burgers with tomato and parsley. Serve with red pepper mayonnaise. Serves 4 to 6.

GLASS NOODLE CHICKEN SALAD

1 teaspoon vegetable oil
½ pound ground chicken
2 ounces cellophane (bean thread) noodles
¼ cup fresh lime juice
1 tablespoon fish sauce (nam pla)
1 tablespoon sugar
2 teaspoons sambal oelek

2 tablespoons vegetable oil
1 large green onion (green part only), chopped
¼ cup chopped fresh coriander
¼ cup chopped fresh mint
¼ cup chopped fresh basil (preferably Thai)
Lettuce leaves

HEAT OIL in medium nonstick skillet over medium heat. Add chicken and cook, breaking up meat with fork, until no pink remains. Using slotted spoon, transfer chicken to a dish; set aside.

Place noodles in heatproof bowl and add very hot tap water to cover them completely. Allow to stand for 10 minutes or until noodles are tender; do not oversoak or noodles will be mushy. Drain very well in footed strainer. Using your hands, toss noodles for a minute or so or until most of the moisture has evaporated; set aside.

To prepare dressing, blend lime juice, fish sauce, sugar, sambal oelek, and vegetable oil in medium bowl until sugar is dissolved.

Toss chicken and noodles in dressing for about a minute to allow mixture to coat noodles evenly. (You can prepare the salad up to this point and refrigerate for up to 2 hours.) Toss in green onion, coriander, mint, and basil. Transfer to lettuce-lined dish and serve at once. Serves 1 to 2.

B*ean thread noodles and ground chicken, tossed with a sweet and spicy vinaigrette, fresh Thai basil, mint, and coriander is my idea of flavor heaven.*
♦ *I serve this as a quick meal in itself or a late-night supper accompanied by a cup of green tea.*

Tacos are fun and festive and messy to eat. They can be filled with whatever one fancies, keeping in mind contrasting textures, colors, and flavors. ◆ When regular tomatoes aren't in season, I substitute ripe cherry or plum tomatoes. ◆ Sambal oelek – an Indonesian condiment of chopped chiles – is available in Asian food shops.

CHICKEN TACOS

2 large (1 pound) ripe tomatoes, diced
1 large garlic clove, finely chopped
½ cup finely chopped red onion
½ cup chopped fresh coriander
1 to 2 tablespoons sambal oelek or chopped jalapeños
¼ teaspoon salt
Freshly ground black pepper
1 tablespoon vegetable oil
2 large garlic cloves, chopped

1 medium onion, chopped
1 pound ground chicken
½ cup chicken stock
½ teaspoon salt
Butter, at room temperature
16 corn tortillas
Grated Cheddar or Monterey Jack cheese
Shredded Boston or iceberg lettuce
Sour cream
1 ripe avocado, peeled, cubed, and tossed with a little lemon juice

To PREPARE SALSA, combine tomatoes, garlic, onion, coriander, sambal oelek, salt, and pepper in medium bowl.

To prepare filling, heat oil in large nonstick skillet over medium-high heat. Add garlic and onion and cook for 2 minutes or until tender. Add chicken and cook, breaking up meat with fork, until no pink remains. Spoon out excess oil and liquid, if any. Stir in chicken stock and salt and bring to a boil. Reduce heat, cover, and simmer for 15 minutes or until stock has evaporated but chicken is still moist. Keep warm.

Lightly butter one side of each tortilla. Heat medium nonstick skillet over medium heat. Add tortilla buttered side down and cook for 30 seconds or until heated and softened. Continue until all are done, stacking them on piece of foil, then enclose; keep warm.

Transfer chicken to warmed serving dish. Put salsa, tortillas, grated cheese, shredded lettuce, sour cream, and avocado in separate bowls.

Each person takes a tortilla and helps themselves to the filling and garnishes, then folds it up and eats it sandwich-style. Makes 16 tacos.

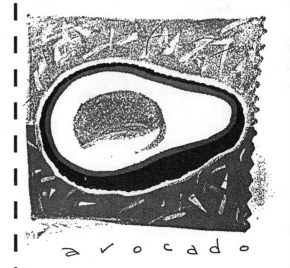

avocado

For chili lovers. ◆ No other accompaniments are necessary – except perhaps some ice-cold beer. The contrasting flavors and textures are provided by crunchy tortilla chips, fresh coriander, green onion, and tomatoes, as well as cooling cheese and sour cream.

CHICKEN CHILI

2 tablespoons vegetable oil	1 teaspoon ground cumin
1 large onion, chopped	6 tablespoons Durkee
10 large garlic cloves, chopped	Frank's Red Hot Sauce
1 pound ground chicken	1 to 2 tablespoons yellow cornmeal
19-ounce can Italian plum tomatoes, undrained	Shredded Monterey Jack or Cheddar cheese
1 cup chicken stock	Sour cream
19-ounce can red kidney beans, drained and rinsed	Chopped fresh coriander leaves
6 tablespoons best-quality chili powder, or to taste	Chopped green onion
1 tablespoon dried oregano	2 ripe tomatoes, coarsely chopped
	Tortilla chips

HEAT OIL in large nonstick skillet over medium-high heat. Add onion and garlic and cook for 2 minutes or until tender. Add ground chicken and cook, breaking up meat with fork, until no pink remains. Stir in tomatoes, including liquid, and chicken stock, reduce heat to medium-low, and simmer for 10 minutes. Add kidney beans, chili powder, oregano, cumin, hot sauce, and cornmeal and simmer 10 minutes or until thickened.

Place cheese, sour cream, coriander, green onion, tomatoes, and tortilla chips in separate bowls. Serve chili in wide bowls; pass the toppings. Serves 6.

ACCOMPANIMENTS

♦ ♦ ♦

Here green beans are cooked in a savory tomato sauce without prior steaming which makes this an easy dish to prepare. Another plus: they can be prepared ahead and reheated. ◆ Don't be alarmed at the length of time the vegetables are cooked: a classic Italian vegetable dish, this is one of those rare occasions when green beans are cooked until quite tender and have lost their bright green color.

GREEN BEANS WITH PEPPERS AND TOMATOES

2 tablespoons olive oil
1 medium onion, thinly sliced
3 large garlic cloves, chopped
¾ pound green beans, trimmed
1 large sweet red pepper, cut into julienne

1½ teaspoons dried basil
1 teaspoon salt
½ teaspoon freshly ground black pepper
19-ounce can Italian plum tomatoes, undrained

HEAT OIL in large nonstick skillet over medium heat. Add onion and garlic and cook for 2 minutes or until tender. Add green beans, red pepper, and basil and cook for 2 minutes. Add salt, pepper, and tomatoes including liquid. Reduce heat to medium-low, cover, and simmer for 30 to 40 minutes or until vegetables are tender. Transfer green beans to a plate. Turn heat to high and cook until sauce is thickened. Return beans to sauce to reheat and serve. Serves 4 to 6.

oarse-grained mustard adds just the right amount of tang to this simple side dish.

GREEN BEANS WITH COARSE-GRAINED MUSTARD

1 pound green beans,
  trimmed
1 heaping tablespoon
  butter
1 heaping tablespoon
  coarse-grained mustard

Salt
Freshly ground black
  pepper

STEAM GREEN BEANS over boiling water for 4 minutes or until crisp-tender and still bright green. Place beans in strainer, then immediately cool under cold running water to set color. (The beans can be prepared up to this point, covered, and refrigerated until serving.)

Melt butter in medium nonstick skillet over medium heat. Add mustard, green beans, salt, and pepper; toss until beans are evenly coated and heated through. Serve at once. Serves 4 to 6.

B

uttery-crisp potato slices are a delicious accompaniment to simple chicken dishes.

OVEN-FRIED POTATOES

¼ cup (2 ounces/½ stick)
   butter
3 baking-type potatoes,
   peeled and sliced
   ¼ inches thick
Salt

PREHEAT OVEN to 450°F.
   Add butter to baking pan just large enough to hold potatoes in one layer (about 13 x 9 inches). Place pan in oven for a few minutes to melt butter. Remove from oven and arrange potato slices in one layer in pan. Sprinkle lightly with salt. Bake for 30 minutes, turning occasionally with large metal spatula, or until potatoes are golden brown and tender. Serves 4.

Serve these potatoes when you're in a hurry and want baked potatoes in a little less time. Besides, they have a more refined appearance than a whole baked potato.

HALVED BAKED POTATOES

2 large baking potatoes,
   well scrubbed and cut in
   half lengthwise

PREHEAT OVEN to 400°F.
   Place potatoes cut side up on baking sheet or right on oven rack. Bake for 40 minutes or until tender and tops have puffed up and formed a golden brown crust. (Be careful not to overcook or potato will dry out.) Serves 2 to 4.

kra is wonderful in this spicy Southern specialty. I like to serve it with fried, roasted, or grilled chicken. ♦ Durkee Frank's Red Hot Sauce is available at most supermarkets.

SPICY OKRA TOMATO STEW

1 tablespoon butter
1 tablespoon vegetable oil
2 large garlic cloves, chopped
1 medium onion, chopped
½ pound fresh okra, trimmed and sliced into ½-inch rounds

19-ounce can Italian plum tomatoes, undrained
1 teaspoon dried thyme
Salt
Freshly ground black pepper
2 tablespoons Durkee Frank's Red Hot Sauce

MELT BUTTER with oil in medium nonstick skillet over medium-high heat. Add garlic and onion and cook for 2 minutes or until tender. Add okra, tomatoes, including liquid, thyme, salt, pepper, and hot sauce and bring to a boil. Reduce heat and simmer for 8 minutes or until thickened and okra is crisp-tender. Serves 4 to 6.

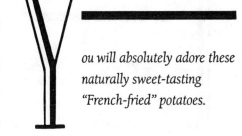

ou will absolutely adore these
naturally sweet-tasting
"French-fried" potatoes.

Sweet-Potato Fries

2 large sweet potatoes,
   peeled
2 tablespoons all-purpose
   flour

Vegetable oil for frying
Salt

Cut potatoes crosswise into ⅛-inch thick slices. Stack a
few slices at a time, then cut lengthwise into ⅛-inch thick
strips, and place on large piece of wax paper. Toss strips
with flour to coat evenly. (Fry immediately: the flour turns
gummy very quickly.)

   Heat 1 to 2 inches oil in large high-sided nonstick or
heavy skillet over high heat to 365°F. (Make sure frying
vessel is large enough: oil foams up a bit during frying.) Fry
potatoes in batches – do not overcrowd pan – for 2 minutes or until crisp but still brightly colored, maintaining
heat between batches. Transfer fries with slotted spoon to
paper towel-lined tray to drain. Immediately sprinkle with
salt to taste. Serve at once. Serves 4.

I love my Caesar salad tangy with lemon and pungent with anchovies. ◆ The secret to an exceptional salad: chill the lettuce and dressing thoroughly and serve promptly after tossing. There's nothing worse than limp, warm lettuce sitting in a warm dressing. ◆ We have friends who are such perfectionists when it comes to serving Caesar salad, they even chill their salad plates and forks to ensure everything stays cool!

CAESAR SALAD

1 large head Romaine
  lettuce
2 large garlic cloves
2 to 6 anchovy fillets
1 tablespoon Dijon
  mustard
1 egg yolk
Juice of ½ medium lemon
  (5 tablespoons)

1 tablespoon
  Worcestershire sauce
Salt
¾ cup vegetable or olive oil
Freshly grated Parmesan
  cheese
Freshly ground black
  pepper

RINSE LETTUCE LEAVES under cold running water, break into large bite-size pieces, and spin dry. Place in plastic bag to chill and crisp for a minimum of 1 hour.

Chop garlic in food processor. Add anchovies and process until puréed. Add mustard and egg yolk and process a few seconds. Add lemon juice, Worcestershire sauce, and a little salt – not too much – the anchovies are very salty. With motor running, drizzle in oil and process until thickened. Taste and adjust seasoning if necessary. Transfer to small bowl, cover with plastic wrap, and chill for a minimum of 1 hour.

To serve, place lettuce in an extra-large bowl. Add dressing and toss until coated evenly. Transfer to an attractive serving bowl. Sprinkle with a little Parmesan cheese and serve extra cheese at the table. Pass the peppermill. Serves 4 to 6.

SPINACH, MUSHROOM, AND SWEET ONION SALAD

5 ounces fresh spinach,
tough stems removed
(about 8 lightly packed
cups)
2 large garlic cloves, finely
chopped
½ teaspoon salt
Freshly ground black
pepper

3 tablespoons tarragon
vinegar
1 tablespoon Dijon
mustard
½ cup vegetable oil
7 thin slices large sweet
white onion
10 medium-large
mushrooms, thinly sliced

RINSE SPINACH under cold running water, break into large bite-size pieces, and spin dry. Place in plastic bag to chill and crisp for a minimum of 1 hour.

Whisk garlic, salt, pepper, vinegar, and mustard in medium bowl until combined. Drizzle in oil in thin stream, whisking until blended. Add onion slices and set aside for several hours for onion to soften, stirring occasionally.

Thirty minutes before serving, stir mushrooms into dressing.

Toss spinach and dressing in extra-large bowl until leaves are evenly coated. Transfer to an attractive serving bowl and serve at once. Serves 4 to 6.

A fresh salad to make when there is an abundance of fresh, peak-of-perfection spinach. ♦ The salad dressing must be made at least four hours ahead for the onion to soften, so plan accordingly. ♦ As a variation, add some crumbled crisp bacon or croutons.

F ast and flavorful, here zucchini are cut into thin julienne
– either with a mandoline (a
professional vegetable cutter)
or by hand – and flash-fried with either
dried basil or thyme. It's up to you to
match the herb with the entrée you are
serving. ◆ Don't grate the zucchini or
they will turn to mush when cooked.

STIR-FRIED ZUCCHINI

1 pound zucchini (about
  3 medium), cut into
  julienne
1 teaspoon salt

1 tablespoon vegetable oil
1 teaspoon dried basil or
  thyme

PLACE ZUCCHINI in a footed strainer. Sprinkle with salt,
toss to combine, and set aside in sink for 20 minutes. Pat
zucchini dry with a clean tea towel – the zucchini strips
must be dry so they don't steam while cooking. Transfer to
a second clean towel if necessary.

    Heat oil in medium nonstick skillet over high heat. Add
zucchini and basil or thyme and stir-fry for 2 minutes or
just until heated through and zucchini is crisp-tender. Do
not overcook. Serves 2 to 4.

FRIED PLANTAINS

2 ripe but firm plantains
Vegetable oil for frying
Salt

TO PEEL PLANTAINS, use a sharp knife and slice off top and tail. Make 3 or 4 lengthwise slits in skin without cutting flesh. Peel back and remove skin. Slice plantains into ¼-inch rounds.

Heat thin film of oil in medium nonstick skillet over medium heat. Add plantains and cook, turning occasionally, for 4 minutes or until tender and golden brown. Transfer to paper towel-lined plate to drain, sprinkle with a little salt; serve at once. Serves 4.

lantains are the green, unripe cousin of the sweet banana. Plantains are never eaten raw, and are enjoyed throughout the Caribbean and Africa. ◆ I serve this as a side dish to Caribbean Curried Chicken (page 54).

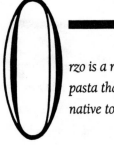

rzo is a rice– or oval-shaped pasta that is a delicious alternative to rice.

ORZO WITH PARMESAN CHEESE

1½ cups orzo
¼ cup (2 ounces/½ stick) butter
¼ cup freshly grated Parmesan cheese plus extra for serving at table

Salt
Freshly ground black pepper

COOK PASTA in plenty of boiling water for 8 minutes or until al dente; drain well. Return to pan, stir in butter, Parmesan cheese, salt, and pepper. Transfer to serving dish and pass extra Parmesan cheese and the peppermill at the table. Serves 6.

A really fresh-tasting side dish – a delicious accompaniment to Mexican entrées or grilled chicken. ♦ This recipe is from my book, _All the Best Mexican Meals_. ♦ The salsa must be served as soon as it is prepared; it loses its sprightliness on standing.

CORN, TOMATO, AND CHILE SALSA

1 cup freshly scraped or partially-thawed frozen corn kernels (about 2 ears corn)

6 ripe cherry tomatoes, coarsely diced

1 large whole green onion, finely chopped

¼ cup pickled sliced jalapeños, chopped

COMBINE ALL ingredients in small bowl and serve at once. Serves 2 to 4.

D*o not use converted or instant rice in this recipe.*

WHITE RICE

1 cup long-grain rice	½ teaspoon salt
1½ cups water	

PLACE RICE in strainer; wash thoroughly by rinsing under cold running water, swirling rice with your hands several times, until water runs clear.

Bring rice, 1½ cups water, and salt to a boil in medium saucepan over high heat. Reduce heat to low, cover, and cook for 25 minutes or until rice is tender and liquid absorbed. Remove from heat and allow to stand for 5 minutes before serving. Remove cover and fluff up with fork if desired. Serves 2 to 4.

utty tasting wild rice is an earthy side dish to chicken. You can make this ahead and reheat it.

WILD RICE

¼ cup (2 ounces/½ stick) butter
1¼ cups chopped white part of leeks (previously well rinsed)

½ pound wild rice (about 1⅓ cups)
1½ cups chicken stock
½ cup dry white vermouth

MELT BUTTER in heavy medium saucepan over medium-high heat. Add leeks and cook for 4 minutes or until tender. Add rice and stir to combine. Pour in chicken stock and vermouth. Bring to a rapid boil over high heat, cover, then turn off heat. Let stand for 1 hour.

Bring rice back to a boil. Cover, reduce heat to medium-low, and cook for 35 minutes or until rice is tender and liquid is absorbed, stirring occasionally. Serves 6.

The combination of chiles, melted Monterey Jack cheese, fresh coriander, sour cream, and rice is absolutely scrumptious. ◆ This recipe is reprinted from my book *All the Best Mexican Meals*.

BAKED RICE WITH CHEESE AND CHILES

2 tablespoons butter
2 large garlic cloves, finely chopped
1 small onion, finely chopped
1 cup Basmati or long-grain rice (not parboiled or converted)
2 cups water

1 teaspoon salt
½ cup sour cream
¼ cup chopped fresh coriander
½ cup pickled sliced jalapeños, coarsely chopped
1 cup grated Monterey Jack cheese

MELT BUTTER in heavy medium saucepan over medium-high heat. Add garlic and onion and cook for 2 minutes or until tender. Stir in rice, add water and salt, and bring to a boil. Reduce heat to low, cover, and cook, stirring occasionally, for 20 minutes or until liquid is absorbed and rice is tender. Transfer rice to a greased 8-inch square glass baking dish and allow to cool thoroughly.

Preheat oven to 425°F.

Stir in sour cream and coriander until combined, then stir in chiles and grated cheese. Bake, uncovered, for 20 minutes or until heated through and lightly flecked with golden brown. Do not overcook. Serves 4.

BASMATI RICE WITH GINGER AND GARLIC

2 tablespoons vegetable oil
5 very thin quarter-size
   slices fresh ginger, very
   finely shredded
4 large garlic cloves, sliced
   into slivers

1 cup Basmati rice
2 cups water
1 teaspoon salt
¼ teaspoon hot red pepper
   flakes (optional)

HEAT OIL in heavy medium saucepan over medium-high heat. Add ginger and garlic and cook for 1 minute or until tender. Stir in rice, then add water, salt, and red pepper flakes. Bring to a boil, reduce heat to low, cover, and cook, stirring occasionally, for 20 minutes or until liquid is absorbed and rice is tender. Serves 4.

Enthusiastically seasoned with garlic and ginger, this rice dish has lots of spunk. Omit the hot red pepper flakes for less heat, if you like, and be sure to shred the ginger as finely as possible. ♦ Basmati rice, an aromatic long-grain rice, is essential for this dish. It is available in Indian, Pakistani, and many Asian and specialty food shops. Ask for aged Basmati for best flavor and fragrance. ♦ Don't bother making this with regular long-grain rice.

*adore this lovely grain –
actually coarse-ground
durum wheat (semolina) –
and find it a wonderful
accompaniment to so many chicken
dishes. I purchase the quick-cooking,
unseasoned variety which is available in
small boxes or sold in bulk in most supermarkets and health food stores.*

Couscous

1¼ cups chicken stock	¼ teaspoon turmeric
½ teaspoon salt	1 cup quick-cooking
2 tablespoons butter	couscous

BRING CHICKEN STOCK, salt, butter, and turmeric to a boil in medium saucepan. Sir in couscous, remove pan from heat, cover, and allow to stand for 5 minutes. Remove cover, stir to fluff up, and serve at once. Serves 2 to 4.

THREE-GRAIN PILAF

2 tablespoons butter
2 garlic cloves, finely
  chopped
1 medium onion, chopped
1 cup mushrooms,
  chopped
2 cups chicken stock
½ cup pearl barley

¼ cup long-grain rice
  (preferably Basmati)
¼ cup coarse-grind bulgur
  wheat
Salt
Freshly ground black
  pepper

MELT BUTTER in heavy medium saucepan over medium-high heat. Add garlic and onion and cook for 2 minutes or until tender. Turn heat to high and add mushrooms. Cook for 4 minutes or until tender.

Add chicken stock, pearl barley, rice, and bulgur; bring to a boil. Cover, reduce heat to low, and cook for 30 minutes or until liquid is absorbed and grains are tender. (Add a little more stock and cook a little longer if grains are not tender.) Add salt and pepper to taste and serve. Serves 4.

*F*eel free to substitute your favorite grains for the ones that I have suggested. ♦ The grains can be found at health food stores and most supermarkets.

INDEX